REVISED EDITION

AARON COPLAND
DUO FOR FLUTE AND PIANO

BOOSEY & HAWKES

 AN IMAGEM COMPANY

DISTRIBUTED BY

 HAL•LEONARD® CORPORATION

7777 W. BLUEMOUND RD. P.O. BOX 13819 MILWAUKEE, WI 53213

www.boosey.com
www.halleonard.com

AARON COPLAND (1900-1990)

Aaron Copland's name is synonymous with American music. It was his pioneering achievement to break free from Europe and create concert music that is characteristically American. At the same time, he was able to stamp his music with a compositional personality so vivid as to transcend stylistic boundaries, making every work identifiable as his alone.

Born in Brooklyn, New York in 1900, Copland set out for Paris in 1920 to study with luminary pedagogue Nadia Boulanger. Among the many vital legacies of his stay in Paris were a growing interest in popular idioms and the insight that there was as yet no American counterpart to the national styles being created by composers from Europe. He became determined to create, in his words, "a naturally American strain of so-called serious music."

Upon his return to America in 1924, his career was launched when Serge Koussevitzky agreed to conduct the Boston Symphony Orchestra in Copland's Organ Symphony. But Copland saw a broader role for himself than mere iconoclast. He sought to further the cause of new music as a vital cultural force. He accomplished this not only by composing, but also by lecturing and writing on new music, and by organizing the groundbreaking Copland-Sessions concerts in New York, which brought many works of the European avant-garde to U.S. audiences for the first time.

As America entered Depression and then war, Copland began to share many of his fellow artists' commitment to capturing a wider audience and speaking to the concerns of the average citizen in those times of trouble. His intentions were fulfilled as works from *Billy the Kid* to *Lincoln Portrait* to the Pulitzer Prize-winning *Appalachian Spring* found both popular success and critical acclaim.

Copland never ceased to be an emissary and advocate of new music. In 1951, he became the first American composer to hold the position of Norton Professor of Poetics at Harvard University; his lectures there were published as *Music and Imagination*. For 25 years he was a leading member of the faculty at the Berkshire Music Center (Tanglewood). Throughout his career, he nurtured the careers of others, including Leonard Bernstein, Carlos Chávez, Toru Takemitsu, and David Del Tredici. He took up conducting while in his fifties, becoming a persuasive interpreter of his own music; he continued to conduct in concerts, on the radio, and on television until he was 83.

Aaron Copland was one of the most honored cultural figures in the history of the United States. The Presidential Medal of Freedom, the Kennedy Center Award, the National Academy of Motion Picture Arts and Sciences "Oscar," and the Commander's Cross of the Order of Merit of the Federal Republic of Germany were only a few of the honors and awards he received. In addition, he was president of the American Academy of Arts and Letters; a fellow of the Royal Academy of Music and the Royal Society of Arts in England; helped found the American Composers Alliance; was an early and prominent member of the American Society of Composers, Authors, and Publishers; served as director or board member of the American Music Center, the Koussevitzky Foundation, the League of Composers, and other organizations; received honorary doctorates from over 40 colleges and universities. In 1982, The Aaron Copland School of Music was established in his honor at Queens College of the City University of New York.

NOTE ON THE REVISED EDITION

The decision was made to prepare a new engraving of Copland's *Duo for Flute and Piano* after determining that the quality of the published first edition engraving was aging. This also afforded an opportunity to reconsider the piece by studying sources. We consulted the composer's manuscripts from The Aaron Copland Collection held in the Library of Congress. The sources were carefully studied and compared to the available edition. As is often the case with works by almost any composer, the main missing sources are the marked pre-publication proofs. Such proofs would typically show decisions made by composer and publication editor as a composition makes its way from manuscript to printed publication. By evaluating the sources and comparing them to the first edition, minor discrepancies were found, almost surely accounting for changes made on the proofs. In addition to a detailed summary of primary and supplementary sources consulted, all such discrepancies can be found in the **Editorial Notes** section which follows on page v. Essentially, these differences amount to a re-constructed estimation of changes made in pre-publication proofs for *Duo for Flute and Piano*. Immediately following the Editorial Notes is an excerpt from *Copland Since 1943*, in which the composer reflects on the genesis and development of the *Duo*.

We would like to thank Boosey & Hawkes, Philip Rothman, The Aaron Copland Fund for Music, the Library of Congress, and Vivian Perlis for her kind permission to reprint the *Copland Since 1943* article.

— Joel K. Boyd, editor
2014

DUO FOR FLUTE AND PIANO (1969-71)

Dedication: To the memory of William Kincaid
Dates of Composition: 1969 to 9 March 1971
First Performance: 3 October 1971, Elaine Shaffer, flute, Hephzibah Menuhin, piano, Settlement Music Festival in Philadelphia, Pennsylvania
First Published: Boosey & Hawkes, Inc., 1971
First Recorded: Elaine Shaffer, flute, Aaron Copland, piano, *Aaron Copland Performs and Conducts Copland*, Columbia Masterworks (M-32737), recorded 11 & 14 December 1972, Vinyl LP released 1974

Commissioned by seventy pupils and friends of William Kincaid, first flutist of the Philadelphia Orchestra from 1921 to 1960.

MUSICAL SOURCES FOR THE REVISED EDITION

Primary Sources

Source A. Manuscript score for flute and piano, 1971; ARCO 94 (Box 110) in The Aaron Copland Collection (Library of Congress); N.B. MS. is in Copland's hand; verified by John Solum.

Editorial commentary: This appears to be Copland's final manuscript score, which was submitted to Boosey & Hawkes for publication.

Source B. Manuscript flute part (by copyist David Walker), 1971; ARCO 94.1 (Box 110) in The Aaron Copland Collection (Library of Congress)

Editorial commentary: This appears to be the final manuscript of the flute part in a copyist's hand.

Source C. *Duo for Flute and Piano* (published edition), 1971; Boosey & Hawkes, Inc. (HL48005922; ISMN 979-0-051-59019-3)

From the original publication: The *Duo for Flute and Piano* was composed on commission from a group of pupils and friends of the late William Kincaid, for many years solo flutist of the Philadelphia Orchestra. Completed in 1971 it was first performed by Elaine Shaffer and Hephzibah Menuhin on October 3rd of that year at the Settlement Music Festival in Philadelphia, Pa.

Supplementary Sources

Source D. Manuscript flute part (ozalid; incomplete – third movement only); ARCO 94.2 (Box 110) in The Aaron Copland Collection (Library of Congress)

From the first page of manuscript Source D: "uncorrected don't use."

Source E. Manuscript pencil draft [original manuscript/early sketches]; ARCO 94.3 (Box 110) in The Aaron Copland Collection (Library of Congress)

From the first page of manuscript Source E: Divertimento Duo Sonatina for fl + piano [with the word "Duo" circled], mvt 1 + 2 + 3, Duo for flute and piano, completed 1970-71, original mms (with sketches); *Notes on second page:* Kincaid memorial, commission suggested by John Solum in honor of Wm Kincaid, Nov. 67 [1967], 12 to 20 min. suggested; [lists an abbreviated summary of movement structure]; *Music page 1 (beginning of Movement I):* original key was A Major [includes arrow pointing up, "Maj. 3rd?"], there's a note stating "Final version transposed up ½ tone (B-flat); *Music page 16 (end of Movement II):* 5 min., July 1 '70.

Editorial commentary: As the first handwritten notes on page one indicate, the title for this work may have been undecided initially. It appears that a few options were considered, ranging from Divertimento and Sonatina to the ultimately selected Duo. Another point of interest is the second page date of November 1967, which suggests that John Solum may have offered the commission to Copland just months after William Kincaid died on 27 March 1967. In the reproduced article from *Copland Since 1943* which follows, the composer relates that up to 1969 the *Duo* only existed in draft form.

Source F. Sketches; ARCO 94.4 (Box 110) in The Aaron Copland Collection (Library of Congress)

Editorial commentary: Source F contains various sketches and fragments related to the *Duo for Flute and Piano*, including: quotes of material used in *Dance Panels* finale (page dated March '44 [1944]) and 3rd Symphony (page dated Jan. 22 '45 [1945]); incomplete sketch of *Duo* scored for woodwind trio: flute, clarinet, and bassoon; as well as early composition drafts for *Duo for Flute and Piano*. In *Copland Since 1943*, the composer confirmed that he incorporated selected material from his 1940s compositions into *Duo for Flute and Piano*. Source F contains what the editors believe to be at least some of these 1940s excerpts.

Source G. Manuscript score (incomplete); ARCO 94.5 (Box 110) in The Aaron Copland Collection (Library of Congress)

From the first page of manuscript Source G: "1st version, incomplete, revised, later version ½ tone higher"

Source H. Miscellaneous pages from score and correction notes, 1971; ARCO 94 misc (Box 110) in The Aaron Copland Collection (Library of Congress)

Editorial commentary: Source H includes typeset corrections [pre-publication process corrections?] and hand-written corrections; a list of where [manuscript?] copies were or still needed to be sent: "send copy to N.B. [?], Elaine S. [Shaffer] – sent mm., B+H [Boosey & Hawkes] (for printing), [Jean-Pierre] Rampal (pd by L of C) – send mm." Although H appears to include some corrections to *Duo* it is difficult to say where they fall in the timeline of the development of the piece. The list of names may be a clue that these corrections were the result of sending pre-publication manuscript copies out for review and feedback, but since it is also listed that Boosey & Hawkes was sent copies for publication preparation, there is no way to be certain.

Source I. Score (publ.) [published edition for flute and piano with editorial markings for violin and piano], 1971; ARCO 94a (Box 110) in The Aaron Copland Collection (Library of Congress)

EDITORIAL NOTES

What follows is a listing of discrepancies found when comparing primary Sources A and B with the published edition, primary Source C. Other sources, listed above, were consulted for historical context and to gain knowledge of the genesis of the work. The result is an estimated re-construction of the markings and small changes by Copland or the Boosey & Hawkes publication editor on the marked publication proofs, which are lost.

Movement I

Flute and Piano Score
M8, 9 – B includes a slur in flute part from downbeat of m. 8 to downbeat of m. 9. A and C do not include a slur.

M10, 11 – A and B do not include a tenuto marking over first note in flute part. C includes the tenuto marking.

M19 – **resume Tempo I** indication begins on last flute note in A, B, and the flute part of C. This tempo indication begins on the downbeat of M20 in the flute and piano score of source C only. As a result, the editors have emended the placement of this indication to begin on last flute note of M19, thus matching sources A, B, and the flute part of C. See note for M141.

M32 (reh. 3) – piano part dynamic is *mf* not *mp* in A. The dynamic is *mp* in C.

M50-56 – there are no pedal markings for the piano in A. Pedal markings appear in C.

M72 – last note in flute part has a staccato in A and B. There is no staccato in C.

M75 – the beat two flute dynamic is *mf* in A, B, and flute part of C. The dynamic is *f* in the flute and piano score of source C only. As a result, the editors have emended this dynamic to be *mf*, thus matching sources A, B, and the flute part of C.

M101 – there are no tenuto markings over the first five flute notes in A, but they do appear in B and C.

M111-115 – there are no pedal markings for the piano in A. Pedal markings do appear in C.

M132, 133 – B does not include a tenuto marking over first note in flute part. A and C include the tenuto marking.

M141 – **resume Tempo I** indication begins on last flute note in A, B, and the flute part of C. This tempo indication begins on the downbeat of M142 in the flute and piano score of source C only. As a result, the editors have emended the placement of this indication to begin on last flute note of M141, thus matching sources A, B, and the flute part of C. See note for M19.

Flute Part
M8, 9 – B includes a slur in flute part from downbeat of m. 8 to downbeat of m. 9. A and C do not include a slur.

M10, 11 – A and B do not include a tenuto marking over first note in flute part. C includes the tenuto marking.

M19 – **resume Tempo I** indication begins on last flute note in A, B, and the flute part of C. This tempo indication begins on the downbeat of M20 in the flute and piano score of source C only. As a result, the editors have emended the placement of this indication to begin on last flute note of M19, thus matching sources A, B, and the flute part of C. See note for M141.

M72 – last note in flute part has a staccato in A and B. There is no staccato in C.

M75 – the beat two flute dynamic is *mf* in A, B, and flute part of C. The dynamic is *f* in the flute and piano score of source C only. As a result, the editors have emended this dynamic to be *mf*, thus matching sources A, B, and the flute part of C.

M101 – there are no tenuto markings over the first five flute notes in A, but they do appear in B and C.

M132, 133 – B does not include a tenuto marking over first note in flute part. A and C include the tenuto marking.

M141 – **resume Tempo I** indication begins on last flute note in A, B, and the flute part of C. This tempo indication begins on the downbeat of M142 in the flute and piano score of source C only. As a result, the editors have emended the placement of this indication to begin on last flute note of M141, thus matching sources A, B, and the flute part of C. See note for M19.

Movement II

Flute and Piano Score
M1 – the right hand piano marking (*r.h. to the fore, bell-like*) does not appear in A. It does appear in C.

M11, 12 – A includes a slur in the right hand piano part which extends from the "B" in M11 to the "F-sharp" in M12. This slur does not appear in C.

M18-20, 26 – there are no pedal markings for the piano in A. Pedal markings do appear in C.

M19 – A and B list the following tempo marking before the metronome marking: **moving forward somewhat**. This marking does not appear here in C.

M22 – there is a *mf* dynamic marking on the upbeat of beat one of the piano part in A. This dynamic marking does not appear in C.

M23-26 – C lists tempo indication as **pressing forward somewhat- - - - holding back - - - - a tempo**. Beginning at M26, A and B list **broaden gradually to - - - -**, ending at the metronome marking in M28.

M34 – there is no tenuto marking over last flute note in A or B. C does list a tenuto.

M43, 44 – B does not list tempo indication **moving to - - - - ♩ = 69**. This tempo does appear in A and C. B lists (♩ **= 69**) at M45.

M51 – A lists the following on downbeat of left hand piano part:

C lists:

M53 – A does not include a roll or an "E" on beat four of left hand piano part. These both appear in C.

M54 – A does not include a roll or an "E" on upbeat of two and beat three of left hand piano part. These both appear in C. A lists a slur in right hand piano part beginning on upbeat of beat two, starting on the initial "E" sixteenth grace note and ending on the beat three "E" quarter note. This slur does not appear in C.

M59 – A lists metronome marking as beginning on beat three of M59. B and C list it in M61.

M61, 62 – A does not include the dynamic marking for a *decrescendo* to *mp* in piano part over the barline. C includes the dynamic marking.

M62, 63 – A includes a *crescendo* marking above right hand piano part on beat four of M62 and a *decrescendo* marking above right hand piano part on beats one through three of M63. These markings do not appear in C.

M64 – A does not include a *decrescendo* marking in piano part. C includes the dynamic marking.

M72, 74 – A includes a tie in right hand piano part which extends from the "B" in M72 to the "F-sharp" tied to beat one in M74. This slur does not appear in C.

Flute Part

M19 – A and B list the following tempo marking before the metronome marking: **moving forward somewhat**. This marking does not appear here in C.

M23-26 – C lists tempo indication as **pressing forward somewhat- - - - holding back - - - - a tempo**. Beginning at M26, A and B list **broaden gradually to - - - -**, ending at the metronome marking in M28.

M34 – there is no tenuto marking over last flute note in A or B. C does list a tenuto.

M43, 44 – B does not list tempo indication **moving to - - - ♩ = 69**. This tempo does appear in A and C. B lists (♩ = 69) at M45.

M59 – A lists metronome marking as beginning on beat three of M59. B and C list it in M61.

Movement III

Flute and Piano Score

M1 – A lists top staff right hand piano chord as half notes. C lists these as quarter notes followed by a quarter rest.

M1 – A lists the expressive marking *sharp, crisp sound* above beat three chord in right hand piano part. This marking does not appear in C.

M1 – A does not list *molto* or (*sempre*) as part of the dynamic marking for beat three right hand piano part. C includes these markings.

M19 – A lists ninth flute note (end of beat three) as "F-sharp" not "A." B and C list this note as "A" not "F-sharp."

M21 – A lists tenuto markings over both "A" quarter notes on beat four of right and left hand piano parts. C does not include these tenuto markings.

M33 – B does not list accents over the first and fifth flute notes. A and C include these accents.

M109 – B does not list **a tempo** and metronome marking. A and C include the tempo indications.

M130 – A lists expressive marking *marc. e stacc.* in flute part. B and C list *non legato*.

M142 – A and B list flute part expressive marking as *don't rush*. C lists the marking as *don't hurry*.

M146 – A and B list an accent over the fourth flute note. C does not include this accent.

Flute Part

M19 – A lists ninth flute note (end of beat three) as "F-sharp" not "A." B and C list this note as "A" not "F-sharp."

M33 – B does not list accents over the first and fifth flute notes. A and C include these accents.

M109 – B does not list **a tempo** and metronome marking. A and C include the tempo indications.

M130 – A lists expressive marking *marc. e stacc.* in flute part. B and C list *non legato*.

M142 – A and B list flute part expressive marking as *don't rush*. C lists the marking as *don't hurry*.

M146 – A and B list an accent over the fourth flute note. C does not include this accent.

EXCERPT FROM
Copland Since 1943
by Aaron Copland and Vivian Perlis
pages 375-77

In draft stage since 1969 had been a work for flute and piano, commissioned by seventy pupils and friends of William Kincaid, first flutist of the Philadelphia Orchestra from 1921 to 1960. After Kincaid died in 1967, John Solum, a former student, organized the committee, and they offered me the commission. Solum and Elaine Shaffer, also a Kincaid pupil, corresponded with me and were most helpful when it came to preparation of the final score, which is dedicated to the memory of William Kincaid. I composed the slow movement first and sent it off to Elaine Shaffer. When I had the second movement in hand, I asked the two flutists to meet with me — after all, this was my first extensive writing for the flute. In one spot, I had asked the flutist to play with a "thin tone" and was told in no uncertain terms that one never invites a flutist to do that! Instead, Solum recommended some harmonic fingerings that gave just the veiled quality I had in mind.

Duo for Flute and Piano is in three movements, with the following indications: Flowing; Poetic, somewhat mournful; Lively, with bounce. My *Duo* is a lyrical piece, in a somewhat pastoral style. Almost by definition, it would have to be a lyrical piece, for what can you do with a flute in an extended form that would not emphasize its songful nature? Lyricism seems to be built into the flute. Some colleagues and critics expressed surprise at the tonal nature of *Duo*, considering that my recent works had been in a more severe idiom; however, the style was naturally influenced by the fact that I was composing for Kincaid's students, not for future generations (although I hoped younger flutists would play *Duo* eventually). Also, I was using material from earlier sketches in my notebooks, and that may have influenced the style of the piece. For example, the beginning of the first movement, which opens with a solo passage for flute, recalls the first movement of my *Third Symphony*.

The first movement is altogether a rather easygoing pastoral sort of movement, while the second uses harmonic and melodic language more akin to my later works, with the principal idea in the flute projecting whole-tone sound similar to the opening of the *Piano Quartet*. The second movement has a certain mood that I connect with myself — a rather sad and wistful one, I suppose. The last movement is lively, with a triadic theme in a free form. The whole is a work of comparatively simple harmonic and melodic outline, direct in expression. Being aware that many of the flutists who were responsible for commissioning the piece would want to play it, I tried to make it grateful for the performer, but no amateur could handle the *Duo* — it requires a good player.

The world premiere of *Duo for Flute and Piano* took place in Philadelphia, performed by Elaine Shaffer with Hephzibah Menuhin, pianist (3 October 1971). The concert was a benefit for Philadelphia's Settlement Music School, and I was pleased to attend. *Duo* was played twice: before intermission and again after. The New York premiere followed at the Hunter College Playhouse with the same players (9 October). *Duo* was warmly received in both cities. I wrote to Chávez (25 December 1971), "I have finished a fourteen-minute *Duo for Flute and Piano*, which was premiered in October, but the musical ideas date from the forties, and so, naturally, the piece is not at all 'avant-garde' in sound. *Eh bien, tant pis!* But it *would* be nice to get some '1970' ideas to work on."

After *Duo* was played for the first time in Boston, Michael Steinberg of the *Boston Globe* wrote (25 January):

> Hearing *Duo* was also an occasion for gratefully remembering how extraordinarily and evenly high Copland's standard of achievement has been. He has composed at greater and lesser levels of musical density, but he has never written inattentively nor, for that matter, without huge signs saying "only by Aaron Copland." The *Duo* is lightweight work of a masterful craftsman. It is going to give pleasure to flutists and their audiences for a long time.

When Elaine and I rehearsed for the Columbia recording of *Duo*, I missed several of my own notes, but Elaine just smiled sweetly and missed none at all! I was shocked when I heard later that she was terminally ill at the time. I am told that our recording was the very last time Elaine ever played. Other fine flutists have taken up the piece from time to time, among them Jean-Pierre Rampal, John Solum, Paula Robison, and Doriot Dwyer. After hearing *Duo*, Leo Smit wrote (19 January 1972), "Flute piece simply lovely, Emilyish with tiny touches of *Piano Fantasy*. Happy for all flutists."

The flute part was edited for violin by Bobby (Robert) Mann of the Juilliard Quartet. He played the first performance of *Duo for Violin and Piano* at the Library of Congress with pianist André-Michel Schub (5 April 1978). The new version was well received; in fact, some critics have preferred the violin arrangement to the flute original.

After Doriot Anthony Dwyer (first flutist of the BSO) played *Duo*, she wrote (4 January 1973), "Everyone I know welcomed your *Duo*, because it was the first composition of yours in a long time, and because of its own lovely spirit." Doriot then asked to arrange my early "Vocalise" for flute and piano. We met and I suggested some adjustments. Doriot had been asking me to compose a work for her instrument for years, and even after *Duo*, she spoke to me about a concerto for flute and orchestra or a chamber piece. I composed neither but was pleased to approve Doriot's flute version of "Vocalise." After the first performance, she wrote (9 April 1973), "Well, the 'Vocalise' is launched! I got the right climax to it, and it was all a great deep pleasure to play. I knew everyone would love it and they did!"

The above excerpt has been reproduced from:
Copland Since 1943
by Aaron Copland and Vivian Perlis
(New York: St. Martin's Press, 1989), pages 375-377
Reprinted by permission.

Duo for Flute and Piano

AARON COPLAND

I

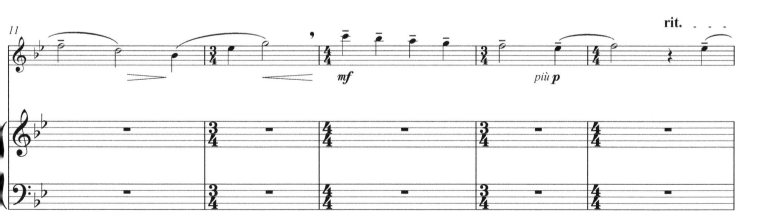

To the memory of William Kincaid

Duo for Flute and Piano

I

FLUTE

Aaron Copland

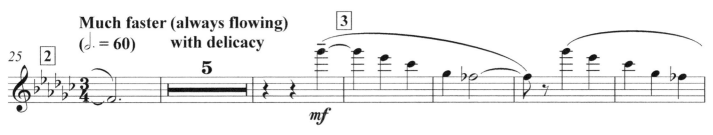

FLUTE

III

Lively, with bounce (♩ = 138)

FLUTE

March 9, 1971

III

March 9, 1971